GRACE-FILLED REFLECTIONS

Joy of My Heart

MARIA GEMMA DEFEO HILOTIN

Grace-Filled Reflections: Joy of My Heart

ISBN: 9798689943879

Cover Print - https://www.vecteezy.com/free-vector/nature

DEDICATION

Right after Mommy's burial in 2018, a rainbow appeared.

When Auntie Beth saw it, she happily told me how I already have a cover for my next book, and Mommy will be happy.

Auntie Beth, this one is for you. Enjoy heaven with Mommy!

Gracita Villanueva Defeo: December 16, 1942 - November 6, 2018
Elizabeth Villanueva Glorioso: March 10, 1938 - August 16, 2020

INTRODUCTION

I started 2020 inspired and encouraged.

To be grateful every day, to see God's work in all that I do, and to always believe that something extraordinary is about to happen - were my primary goals.

And then the COVID-19 pandemic took over.

And life drastically changed.

As you flip through the pages of this book, I hope you would respond to each of the reflective questions as well and find it in your heart to continue to appreciate even the littlest things and remain grateful.

Because, as always, despite the challenges, sorrow, problems and concerns, God's grace abounds even more.

WHAT IS YOUR PRAYER?

The other side of fear is a quiet reflection that everything happens for a reason.

In the silence of our hearts, let us remember to follow the inner voice calling us to keep calm because, as always, God will make a way.

* * *

Lord, please allow a ray of bright light to appease our hearts as we learn our lessons. We pray!

WHAT MOVES YOU?

I am a work in progress.

I am grateful for life's challenges.

And I know it is God who is prodding me to do more and to be more as He fulfills the dream within me.

* * *

Let's do-be-do-be-do!🩶

WHAT DO YOU BELIEVE IN?

Deo Volente. God willing. Daddy taught me that phrase in my elementary days, InShallah! And it has become my favorite ever since.

Daddy told me we could only make plans and act on them, but God has to OK the results we want.

I pass on that phrase to people I meet, asking for prayer and petitions or sharing their dreams, wants, and needs.

Yes, all things are possible, if God is willing.

I love that I have to fully rely on God's providence, guidance, and will because it guarantees that come what may, God is with me.

* * *

God is good! 🖤

WHAT GIVES YOU CONFIDENCE?

When Jesus said, "Rise, pick up your mat and walk!", to me, it feels like He was saying, "Go ahead and make your dreams come true!"

* * *

Awesome God!🖤

WHAT'S YOUR DREAM?

I admire people who are bold and fearless in shouting out their dreams to the whole world. It takes a lot of courage to reveal your heart's desires to social media, and it takes a lot too, to make it happen.

People ask me this question often, and as always, I would shy away from answering it.

Maybe: I am far too careful, allowing negative people to spoil my goals for me. Perhaps, I treasure my plans so much that I would rather keep them to myself and let my results do the talking.

Maybe, it's time to open up.

* * *

Free me from fears, oh Lord.🖤

WHO FIGHTS YOUR BATTLES?

The TV was loud when I woke up this morning. My husband Dennis was very focused on watching *Breaking Bad.*

I gave up on watching TV series since I tend to get addicted and binge-watch! It's counterproductive for me.

At noontime, I went to a training and got back home around 7:00 PM only to find Dennis at the same location watching the same TV series! I didn't comment when I would usually do.

I kind-a gave up on picking fights with him too!

Around ten in the evening, he turned off the TV and went to bed. Out of the blue, he said, I'm happy to see you change. Thank you. I know you are controlling yourself!

* * *

Changes do matter. Thank you, God. 🖤

WHO DO YOU LISTEN TO?

"Prayer is not only talking to God but listening to Him as well."

I closed the book and prepared myself to listen, but my mind told me to send messages to three of my friends, and I did. While chatting with them, two more sent messages. In between chats were phone calls from Dennis asking my plans for today. And then, another urgent phone call.

At every break, I tried to listen, but to no avail. So I did my errands instead.

While driving, I said, I was supposed to listen to You, yet I never did. But, in the silence of my heart, God whispered, "Yes, you did... remember the messages and the phone calls?"

* * *

Help me listen, oh God. 🖤

WHO DO YOU FOLLOW?

Sometimes, I can be indifferent to other people's sufferings and struggles. I underestimate people's feelings. I couldn't care less about sad situations until it hits home and hard.

Our prayers are powerful. Positive thoughts, well-wishes, and simple acts of kindness will go a long way. These are good habits with which to begin.

* * *

Let me follow Your lead, oh Jesus. 🖤

WHO LOVES YOU?

"Oh Lord, when things are hopeless, and prayer is difficult, help us to simply trust in You and leave the outcome in Your hands."

Mommy wrote that prayer on the first page of the book she sent me in 2014. The prayer became more meaningful when Mommy got sick in 2016. It was a total surrender to His will.

Mommy had weak lungs since she was young and had been taking prescriptions ever since. When the doctors gave up on her, our family agreed that she wouldn't take any more drugs except for her vitamins to let her body heal on its own.

Through God's grace, she lived two more years with more answered prayers for the family.

* * *

May we learn to see you, Lord, in blessings and difficulties.
♥

WHAT'S YOUR PURPOSE?

"You're as good as your last sale." I heard this line a lot when I worked in sales and marketing. In a way, it has challenged me to do more.

Selling is an exciting adventure for me, but I was never successful!

And I won't ever be. Because no matter what I do, what company I join, or goods I sell, if I don't align it to God's purpose for me, then it is all in vain.

Interestingly, life's blessings continue to flow when we serve His purpose.

* * *

Allow me to serve you, Lord.

WHAT AMAZES YOU?

"Please give me a chance to talk to everybody, so I can tell God's goodness and share with them all the miracles He has given!" said Tito, who just had Anointing of the Sick, last night.

We initiated the prayers, but he ended up praying and sharing his wisdom with us instead.

At ten in the evening, he was sharing his life stories starting from the year 1972!

For the first time since we've known him, he was suddenly filled with passion and joy to share God's word!

Amidst the laughter and happy chat with Tito was a mixed feeling of awe and amazement in God's manifestation of His love and mercy.

* * *

For Your merciful surprises, thank You, God.

WHAT DO YOU DO?

When I was working at the New Mexico Public Education Department, friends would ask about what Dennis does for a living. I'd proudly say he's a custodian (a fancy word for janitor).

What the world regards as a prestigious or a lowly job does not matter to me. It is a job.

One's perception matters. And it is not what "others think of us" that is important. Sometimes it is not even what "we think of ourselves and the world around us" that is of the essence, but what matters the most is what God thinks about it all.

* * *

Let me know Your ways, oh God.

WHO'S YOUR PRIORITY?

One night, before the year ended, I was surprised when I suddenly uttered, "God, we need to talk," and yet fell into a sound sleep after that.

It wasn't until today that I was reminded again of how God will plant a seed of longing, yearning, and desire into our hearts so we will continue to pursue Him.

I thank God. We are all works-in-progress. We may be in different starting points, routes, or points of view, but I think, as long as we have the same #1 priority, God (however you perceive Him to be), we're OK.

* * *

Thank you, God! 🖤

WHO JUDGES YOU?

"Ching Zung Tsian Tsung? Zung Tsung!" the student mockingly shouted in the hallway as we walked past him, his group laughed out loud. He was mimicking how Chinese people speak; they thought we were Chinese! It was our first week on the job, in the school with 100% Black Americans.

I looked him in the eye and smiled.

I think there were a couple more instances of bullying, but instead of defending ourselves, we'd be kind and take it all in.

And then it stopped.

Because one day, we told one of the students in the group that Jackie Chan is our cousin, and we all know karate! Hehe.

The air changed after that.

* * *

At all times, please be our judge, Lord. 🖤

WHO'S YOUR GO-TO PERSON?

One day, out of the blue, Mommy said that whenever she'd miss Daddy, or there were issues about their differences in religion or other matters, she would not run to her friends, sisters or brother, or even her mom. Mommy said she would go directly to the Blessed Sacrament to cry her heart out. There, she finds peace and joy.

I didn't know until now that Mommy's stories have directly impacted how I go about life. I have yet to fall in love with visiting the Blessed Sacrament. But praying and surrendering all my concerns to Jesus is always my number 1 too.

* * *

For the insights, I am grateful, Lord. 🖤

WHO MAKES YOU LAUGH?

For the first time in 17 years, we decided to take a weekend trip without the kids.

Dennis woke up early to put things together at home, and then we left at 4:30 AM for the nine hour trip. It was a pleasant trip. I slept while he drove all the way!

He said yes to all my plans. It was a great date.

Until he said, "Pay for my services, in dollars!" 😄

* * *

Lord, let me grow in your love always. 🖤

WHAT'S YOUR FAVORITE RESPONSE?

When asked to serve, give or do what I felt was a significant task for me, my favorite answer has always been "NO, I can't, Nope, Nahhh, Not me." And every time people would stop asking me for anything, I'd feel joyful!

There was always a sense of victory when people would embrace my "big no" with open arms. It made me happy not to be bothered. I would think, "What a peaceful life!"

But God threw me a curveball through Dennis.

I thought to shut people out, making myself unavailable, and excusing myself made me happy because that has served me for a long time. When I learned to stop being afraid of the word YES and put my YES in action, I also learned to submit to Dennis. And in doing so, I've also realized how generous and unselfish he is.

I realized I had it all backward all along.

I thank God for His patience, love, and mercy to help me understand that my life has evolved, and with its unfolding, I have to change so that I could be the me He has always wanted me to be.

* * *

Yes, Lord.

WHAT MAKES YOU CRY?

I was sharing with Mommy, over a long-distance call, how the month was almost over, and still, I hadn't found work yet. By that time, I had already resigned from my teaching job in Lucena and decided to work in Manila, thinking it would be easy!

I was expecting her to say, "You can do it!" to encourage me or "You shouldn't have resigned without another job yet," to blame my decisions, but instead, she said, "Just go home."

My heart was already heavy with the stresses of looking for work, but to hear her response made my tears fell some more. I told her, "No, I can do this! Please pray for me!"

True enough that week I got a job!

Our words can break or make us. But, what's more powerful are the words we kept hidden in our hearts, our prayers.

* * *

I am grateful for Your embrace, Oh God!

WHO DEFENDS YOU?

The priest at St. John Vianney church would recite this prayer after every Sunday mass.

"St. Michael, the Archangel, defend us in battle, be our protection against the malice and snares of the devil. We humbly beseech God to command him, and do thou, O Prince of the Heavenly Host, by divine power thrust into hell satan, and the other evil spirits who roam through the world, seeking the ruin of souls. Amen."

Although I would rather not think of the "malice and snares of the devil," it exists in different forms, shapes, and sizes, and unfortunately, it targets our minds first.

* * *

Lord, please keep our hearts and minds pure with Your love, goodness, and mercy. 🖤

WHO WAITS FOR YOU?

I decided to spend a month in the Philippines in 2018 to be with my parents. A month after I left, Mommy passed on. While I was there, one night, I went out with friends. At 11:00 PM my phone rang. It was Daddy. I forgot to let them know that I'd be going home late and got some good reminders about it.

When I was finally home, I checked on Mommy's room to find her still awake. She asked where I had been and told me that she couldn't sleep because I was still out. I honestly thought that since I was already an adult with children of my own, they wouldn't worry anymore. Oops, wrong assumption!

I came home very late today for some trip out of town. When I walked through the altar after turning the lights on, I found Mommy's candles lighted. I had goosebumps. I woke Dennis up and asked if he turned them on; he said, "No, maybe Mommy was waiting for you, so she turned it on," and he went back to sleep.

It is amazing how in life or even death, the best gift we can give is still our "presence."

Good night, Mommy.

* * *

Embrace Mommy, Lord.

WHAT MAKES YOU GROW?

When we answered God's call to "bloom" where He "planted" us, He also provided new beautiful friends who will be part of our journey towards Him.

It's been four years now since we joined CFC.

And with life's twists and turns is a joyful experience of God's tight embrace.

* * *

Thank you, Lord, for blessing us with life-giving friendships. Allow us to grow in You always.

WHAT ARE YOU UNWILLING TO DO?

What are we unwilling to do to make our dreams come true?

If we continue to make excuses, we fail to move forward. We end up where we are.

* * *

Lord, give us the heart to be more like You.

WHAT SECRETS DO YOU KEEP?

A t an early age, I learned that I can't please everybody. So, I no longer try.

But, I like it best when people direct their issues with me than with everybody else. Feedback is the best gift we can give to each other, way better than gossiping.

First, it opens up communication lines and solves the problems, and second, we both grow.

* * *

Lord, help us to purify our intentions. You said everything hidden would be made manifest, and every secret thing will be made known. 🖤

WHAT KEEPS YOU BUSY?

Dennis being an H4 visa holder for six years, with no authorization to work legally here in the US, devoted his time taking care of us, and at some point, on getting scraps to put to good use.

I love the times when he's busy. Because it means his mind has no time to wander, to worry, to be afraid.

* * *

Please envelop us with Your white mantle of protection, Lord, to weather all mind viruses. Consume us with Your love, always.🖤

WHAT MAKES YOU SUCCESSFUL?

I remember two buses full of excited "edutainers" en route to Laguna one Saturday a long time ago...

The manager told us we would get 8,000 pesos commission if we closed a computer deal! Two by two, we went knocking on homeowner's doors on foot, from nine in the morning until nine at night. On our way home, I couldn't help but smile. 🏆

* * *

Lord, let us always remember that obeying You is the real success. 🖤

WHO IS YOUR GOLIATH?

I've learned to look at problems as learning opportunities. When we overcome those, we will be ready for the next level. Like in a video game, it will give us more breathtaking adventures!

Well, a few times during the first seven years in our marriage, Dennis was my Goliath. 😂

Anytime he would mention about breaking up 😳, I'd respond with, "If that makes you happy, I'll support you all the way!" 🤭

I guess it pays to be supportive because it unlocked more happy surprises! 📸

* * *

Notable is Your solutions, Lord! I'm grateful!💜

WHY NOT GIVE UP?

And why shouldn't we give up on our dreams?

* * *

… because if we see it in our minds, we'll hold it in our hands someday. Believe it! 🖤

WHAT'S YOUR SUPER POWER?

I remember one of my grandmother's sisters, Mama Vering and her gift of healing.

When any of us, her grandchildren, were sick, she would gladly visit us, do her rituals, and then we'd get better.

I grew up not doubting her powers. And I think the belief in the gift that God gave her made more people seek her touch, presence, and healing.

I miss our beautiful grandmothers.

* * *

Lord, please allow our words, presence, and touch brings healing to those who need it.

WHAT DO YOU LOVE TO DO?

I miss me.

I love that God has His ways of bringing us back to Him. If it weren't for the reflective journey that I embarked on, I wouldn't realize that I miss me. I mean, I miss writing.

I felt closest to myself whenever I write. The words would flow when I quiet myself and surrender control. But I was more impressed by the feeling of joy at the end of every piece.

I haven't been writing for years, and it felt like the flow of inspiration has stopped. Well, either that or I have become more engrossed with life and living that it has become a burden.

I made a mistake. It wasn't just me that I felt closest to whenever I write, but the source of all inspiration. The one I really long for the most.

Now, I'm back, and this time it all makes sense as I see writing in a new light. I now understand why I feel joy every time, and it's because I know God is embracing me.

So, here I am, writing again to give back, to love back.

And as I am blessed, I hope you will be blessed as well.

* * *

Thank you God for bringing me to the fold.

WHAT IS LOVE?

I looked at my clients' faces uncertainly. The older woman could undoubtedly be the man's mother! I checked their birthdays for the second time - the woman was born in 1962; the man in 1980! I stared at them again, puzzled at what I was seeing. Are they "joking" me? Are they telling the truth?

I remember the episode of MMK last week about the older woman who married a younger man...

Unable to stop myself from asking, I blurted, "He's your husband?" and to the man, "She's your wife?" They both nodded. I smiled, amazed by love.

* * *

Let Your love fill our minds and hearts, all the days of our lives, Lord.

WHAT ARE YOUR MOTIVES?

I've concluded that I won't be able to please people ever! They will always have something to say and judge as if they know it all?

And then I looked closer, and for some reason, I just thought, does it matter if I win the argument, if I hold on to my grudge?

God sees what is in our hearts. He sees it all. That's all that matters.

* * *

Help us purify our thoughts and intentions, Lord, so that we can serve You more.

WHAT MAKES YOUR HEART BEAT FASTER?

At least where we live in the US, it is unusual to hear cars honking. It means something when you blow the horn.

Last night, Dennis merged to the left and got beeped at! He honked back! Tsk tsk, the other driver doesn't want to give when he should and he could.

I've seen many drivers like that. Even when they see your signals, they wouldn't care. They would cut you to drive ahead, and then you all meet at the stop sign.

Ah, the "road test" of loving God.

* * *

Please reign in our hearts, Lord, wherever we are.

WHO'S YOUR GOD'S GIFT?

I t was a rollicking adventure when Aleli and I opened ourselves to finding the One.

Armed with courage and faith, I met my first date, and to my surprise, it was fun! I especially like eating out at excellent restaurants, free! Lol!

I was having fun dating guys until I heard a voice loud and clear in my heart, "He's my gift for you!"

I looked at Dennis in the eye and thought, "Wow, that's weird!" But the voice kept on shouting the same words, and my heart beat unusually fast.

* * *

When we open ourselves to love, we open up to You, Lord.♥

WHAT CAN YOU CONTROL?

Last-minute, we drove to El Paso, Texas, for the first time yesterday. Mostly, to take advantage of the long weekend, take a break from routine, and visit the Outlet Shoppes.

The plan was to visit and "hopefully" not buy anything! I was doubtful it will happen, with teenagers in tow, knowing we can all be impulsive buyers.

But, 'amazing' happened! We went in and out of excellent shops admiring the material things and buying none. 🛍️

* * *

Lord, lead our minds to choose You, daily. 💜

WHAT DO YOU WORRY ABOUT?

One summer, I rode a horse for the first time.

I thought it was easy until I was on it!

Oh my, instead of going with the flow, I resisted so much!

And because of panic, I tried to control the horse's movement even if the caretaker was holding the rein the whole time.

My body ached the next day.

Ah, when will I understand? God's got me!

* * *

Forgive the many times we failed to trust in You, Lord. 🖤

WHAT IS IMPORTANT?

I always mock Dennis because he loves to watch TV series that are full of drama and negativity. Over and over again, I always remind him to be mindful of the scenes. And to listen for the words that the characters are uttering.

I didn't know I got into his system because one day he saw me watching "Love Thy Woman"... and then he heard the lines from each scene... and loudly shouted, "Stop watching that! You know it's all hatred, bullying, and wrongdoings! It will only pollute your mind!"

* * *

We may not yet be where we want to be, Lord, but we are no longer where we used to be. Thank you for the baby steps.

WHAT CONSUMES YOUR MIND?

While shopping for exchange gifts last Christmas, I suddenly thought about the gift I want to receive a "kitchen drying mat."

And guess what I received for my exchange gift? Exactly that! Weird.

Amazing where our thoughts can lead us! Now, if only we can elevate our thinking beyond the worldly to eternal, that will be the day!

* * *

Lord, grant us the grace to seek You first. 🖤

WHAT IS THE BEST ACT?

While Mommy was perfectly content that we lived in a small house at the back of their home, my heart bled for change.

I was so determined to steer the course of our lives. To trigger change, I brought the kids with me to get our passports started.

And to let God know I'm serious about my decision, I bought a suitcase!

And then the "miracle" happened.

* * *

For everything that You allow to happen in our lives, Lord, thank you!

WHAT CAN'T YOU BELIEVE?

The math test was the most challenging of all the tests I took to get me to highly qualified teacher status years ago.

Although it was only an option and not a required test for me, I exerted more for that test than all other criteria, making it one of the most memorable!

My results? My score was two points higher than the passing rate - the sweetest of all the ratings I've ever received!

* * *

Ignite our hearts to believe in You, Lord, with no ifs or buts.
♥

WHAT IS FASTING?

I just saw Dennis take a whole plate of rice and fried anchovies! I told him, hey, that's your second plate, and you're supposed to fast!

Later in a gathering, he saw me eating and asked why I was eating again. I said, No, no, this is just my second meal!

Wahhh, temptations abound!

* * *

Until we become at peace with You, oh God, we will continue to compare, judge, and criticize. We are sorry.

WHAT'S YOUR WISH?

E very Holy Week, I'd pray for love to come my way. I was single then and never had a relationship.

Be careful what you wish for, so they say because, indeed, it came true!

I met him on Holy Monday. I attended mass with him on Holy Tuesday. I talked over the phone on Holy Wednesday. He came home with me to Lucena to meet Mommy on Maundy Thursday.

And on Easter, we saw each other again!

And that night, after a beautiful movie, out of the blue, I told him, "You're my boyfriend, already!"

But before I even got excited about what was about to unfold, he called that same night before I was about to sleep, to tell me he was leaving the country the next day to fulfill a work contract for a year.

. . .

*A*h, my one Holy Week love story!

* * *

But, more than anything, Jesus, thank You again and again for Easter. 🖤

WHAT IS VALUABLE?

M y excitement turned to fear of the unknown when I read the email. I'd been praying for this, and it seemed God is answering it positively.

But instead of spending time to thank God solely, I also Googled Virgo in 2020 to confirm what astrology had to say.

Ah, such a fool.

* * *

You already know what we need before we even ask You, God. Please forgive our folly.🩶

WHAT TO FIND?

...In the ordinary and simple moments

... in the journey more than the destination

... in the deeper discovery of yourself

Find joy!

* * *

Always!🖤

WHAT MAKES YOU FEARLESS?

I put on my blinders yesterday to keep me from becoming distracted or panicked by everything that is happening to our world.

I deliberately focused on my project at hand, but at 1:45 am, I still couldn't figure it out!

I gave in to sleep instead.

* * *

Lord, we know when all else fails, You won't.

WHAT MATTERS MOST TO YOU?

"Grace! Gracee! Graaaace!" The loud voice awakened me. It was calling Mommy's name. I heard Mommy open the door. I sleepily waited in bed, trying to take in as much information as I could. In a panicked voice, my mom's sister informed her of an impending eruption of the volcano in our city. If the volcano erupts, we would all drown, she said.

I went outside and saw my brothers ready to peep at the window (Daddy was working abroad when that happened), but Mommy just about entered the house and closed the door. Without any foreword, she said, "Go back to sleep and pray. No one leaves the house. If it happens, we die, we all die together." Without any discussion, we all silently went to our rooms.

Mommy has always been our leader. We take her words to heart. That night when I went back to sleep, I pondered on what Mommy said — to pray and sleep. Given, we don't have private transportation to escape. Still, if the news was real, I was pretty sure there were other ways to save our family. Being the oldest child, I knew I could dispute her decision; I could always complain and tell her we had other choices, but how could I, when Mommy, without any hint of doubt, anxiety, or worry, told us to pray and sleep.

And so I did, peacefully.

The next day, we heard, "The news was fake."

* * *

Jesus, teach us to sleep soundly, as You did during the storm, too, trusting God wholeheartedly. 🖤

WHAT KEEPS YOU GOING?

There are no absolutes. Nothing is predestined or set in stone.

And it's not as if we could be bored enough, feel frustrated enough, or complain enough that our lives would suddenly turn around. I don't think it works that way.

Life is fragile.

And to wake up every day grateful, matters.

* * *

Lord, be part of the transformations in our lives. We surrender.

WHAT IS LUCKY?

As we were walking out of the casino after enjoying dinner, we saw people crowding this lady.

I took a peep too!

The flashing animations and celebratory winning jingles must have been a joy to her sight and music to her ears as onlookers oohed and aahed, and shook their heads.

* * *

She must have felt fortunate indeed but definitely nothing compared to when You will welcome us back in Your arms, Lord. 🖤

WHAT IS A MAGICAL MOMENT?

As my journey continues, I know more magical moments will happen as long as I connect the dots and understand the purpose. Some connections may be short, some long, some recently started, some would be ignored, and some have stopped.

But when I look at how far I've traveled and the path I am still on, I give God glory.

I hope you, too, would find connections and magical moments and feel... Him.

* * *

Thanks for the love, Lord.🖤

WHAT IS TRUE?

I want to think that the thing we're dealing with right now is not by chance.

It's the beginning of the most exciting transformation of our lives so far.

* * *

Lord, allow us to find calm in the chaos.🖤

WHAT IS DIFFICULT?

For every trial, difficulty, and disappointment, let's ask ourselves, "What does this create an opportunity for?"

The message may not be as loud and clear, and we may find ourselves with more resentment, anger, or impatience, but remember those too, are gifts, like everything else. EVERYTHING else.

* * *

Allow our minds to see beyond what our sight can see, Lord.

And who knows? If we look close enough, we may find —in disguise— more love, healing, and fulfilled dreams instead. 🩶

WHAT'S YOUR FILTER?

I have recently been catching myself, saying, "Stop it!" to the voice that whispers in my head. Usually, I'd go with the flow to accept whatever it told me. Eager to follow its path, I'd join in. Even if it led me to a treacherous route, I was open, willing, and victim.

Ahh, I have learned to filter since then.

Any whisper of negativity, shame, tease, put-downs, criticisms, and the like, I have learned to stop it the moment I hear it. I now have guards securing the gates of my heart, checking every thought, keeping that negativity from getting in.

The guards, I have learned, have to be awake and aware continually. But there are times when they are hungry and tired, that they tend to give in most of the time and allow temptations and all the other spirits to get in.

And it's not favorable.

The question isn't about what I regularly do every day, but am I learning from any of it? Because until something makes sense, until something clicks and hits me in the head to awaken me, then I would go round and round like in a merry-go-round until it's ready to stop, and I remain the same.

And I don't want that.

* * *

Keep me in Your embrace, oh God. 🖤

WHAT DOES IT MEAN TO BE STILL?

What does it mean to be still?
to stay put

to stop striving

to stop struggling

to relax

to chill

to stop running

to stop fighting

to calm down

to stop worrying

to quiet our mind

to live quietly

to stop trying to control things

to stop figuring things out

to wait

to find contentment

to let go and let God

* * *

We run to You, Lord. We are safe in Your arms. Please
envelop us with Your presence. ♥

WHO LOVES YOU?

Don't let your hearts be troubled, says the Lord. Trust that I am with you, until the end of time. Open your hearts to me and allow me to love you more and more!

* * *

Hugs 🖤

WHAT BOGGLES YOUR MIND?

I watched different conspiracy theories about the cause of the virus, and for a minute, it felt right almost to the point of happiness to have something or someone to blame.

And then suddenly I stopped; what if they were wrong?

Blaming is counterproductive. And overthinking isn't good either. We went for a walk instead.

* * *

Lord, I learned that if we must look back, let us do so forgivingly. If we must look forward, let us do so prayerfully. But the wisest thing we can do is to be present in the present gratefully.

No matter what, Lord. Thank You. 🖤

WHAT IS CHANGE?

Dennis unexpectedly confessed to me, "God answered my prayers. because, after all these years, you've finally changed!"

Shocked, I babbled, "No, you changed! You changed the way you look at things, so the things you looked at changed!"

He gazed at me for a few seconds and blurted, "What?!"

* * *

Thanks for changing our hearts, Lord!

WHAT ARE YOUR CHOICES?

We fall, we rise, we make mistakes, we learn...
We keep ourselves busy.

We extend our patience.

We hope for a silver lining.

We pray more.

* * *

Thank you, Lord, for removing our blinders and allowing us to see the options and choices on our plate.

WHAT CAN YOU OFFER?

Mommy would always tell us to accept the first job offer, not resign until we have another job, and never share our plans and goals with anyone until they are achieved.

I don't know where she got those ideas.

But, I followed her lead.

I accepted my first job offer. I try not to resign until I know my next step. And I have always debated, argued, and pushed against sharing my plans and goals with anyone but God and myself, and weirdly, Mommy's words will always end up correct.

* * *

We offer all our plans and goals to You, Lord. 🖤

WHAT IS GOOD?

A friend once said, "I cook what I want to eat!"

It was shocking to me because, in my case, we eat what I can cook.

And given my skills, there's not a lot that I can put together.

Now, with shelter-in-place, I've put all my excuses down the drain and became a risk-taker chef! Haha.

* * *

We appreciate You, Lord, because even in life's littlest and simplest things, You are there. 🖤

WHAT'S YOUR ME-TIME?

The walk I had this morning was pretty special.

I realize that I can make walking my "me" time to listen, reflect, and retreat. So I did.

I shut down the inner noise and thanked God for the day. And I walked in silence.

And then the beautiful messages came in the quiet voice I hear in my heart, one word at a time, loud and clear.

The first of the messages was this:

There's no need to justify. Let it be!

As planned, I stopped to write it down. I didn't process any of it or connect it to anything. I continued walking.

As I turned onto the next street, another message came, this one longer:

By the grace of God, you will be blessed. Continue planting the seeds. Be steadfast. Do not be wary or concerned. Just do the work at hand.

I jotted the words down and felt the cool breeze and the heat of the sun on my face. It was midday, and I love the perfect combination.

But halfway through the route, my mind suddenly got distracted, and I was side-tracked. After sending the last text, I realized either I allow my walking time to be sacred and purposeful or not bother doing it at all.

I took a deep breath and allowed myself to listen once more.

The last message came:

Write from the heart. Do not seek the adulation of men. Please Me. Only Me. I love your grace-filled messages, and I love that you are growing in spirit.

I closed my eyes and felt God's love as I headed home.

* * *

For the heartfelt messages, God, thank You! 🩶

WHAT'S YOUR WORRY?

"Why do you always have solutions? You always think as if everything is light and bright?!" I wasn't able to respond at once since Dennis turned off the phone, obviously upset.

I also decided not to call back and instead took time to think about what he said. He was angry because I do not worry as he does? Huh? Is that a real problem?

Men are from Mars, Women, from Venus!

* * *

Dear Lord, thank you for loving us for who we are. We are not worthy, but You love us just the same.

WHAT FILLS THE VOID?

They said you have to eat whatever you want, especially if you are pregnant. So, while I was pregnant, I'd always be thinking of food to eat. It must be all-in-the-mind.

But one day, I asked for red bananas to test if Dennis would be able to deliver. I was surprised when he brought me some! I didn't know they existed! My heart was full.

* * *

For filling our earthly needs, thank you, Jesus. Please also satisfy the void we feel in our hearts. 🖤

WHAT DO YOU WANT?

I remember being asked by one of the job interviewers a long time ago, "What do you want?" and I couldn't answer her.

The time allowed me to be more retrospective and realized how God had given me everything I want regardless.

And if asked the same question again today? Oh, I know in sacred details, but I'd still be tongue-tied! Lol.

I thank God I've made friends with fear (even if I still fear it) and embraced the beauty of change, and warmed my heart to infinite possibilities (even if anything can happen, really)!

Because to make 'it' happen... I am taking a leap of faith!

* * *

May God bless the desires of our hearts.

WHO FORGIVES YOU?

There are many times in my life that I have failed to walk in the shoes of others. I have become comfortably lazy and selfishly self-assured that I have missed the opportunities to nurture and cultivate relationships.

But the feeling was also vastly different because even as I hold my breath, I could feel the love, understanding, and forgiveness emanating from His heart. And in an instant, great warmth replaced the feelings of unworthiness.

And surprisingly, I love that.

* * *

I love you, Lord.

WHAT DO YOU DESERVE?

It makes me happy to see you happy with even the littlest gifts. I know you deserve more. It's coming soon — wait for it! — Jesus

* * *

Let's keep the faith, everyone!💜

WHAT MAKES YOU LEARN?

I was cursing myself after the test! How could I be so dumb?!

I think it took me an hour to get over.

After an hour, I realized no matter how many times I tell myself how stupid I was for pressing the wrong button, nothing would change what happened. I told myself, I can only learn from the experience and that I would simply need to make decisions wisely next time.

Ummm... until now I am still trying to make better decisions. Hahaha.

The good news is that I do not curse myself anymore. Instead, I forgive myself. I learn again and again, and I move on.

* * *

Next...💚

WHY CRY?

My father looked at me and asked if everything was OK. I told him, 'Of course, I just need to wash my eyes.'

I couldn't tell him the story.

He nodded his head and allowed me to succumb to my emotions. He didn't ask any more questions.

And that was the best gift he has ever given that day, his silent presence.

I cannot undo what was done, I can only learn from it. That has been my battle cry even when I was younger. I can only move forward. I can only look at solutions, and not the problem.

But at that moment, I felt I had to recollect my thoughts so I could pin on what I needed to change and learn from.

As I gathered memories I allowed my tears to wash away all feelings of pity, envy, anguish and resentment of self and overwhelming experiences.

I allowed my tears to set me free from unwanted feelings and I allowed my tears to open up a new world of insights and feelings of love, hope, peace.

My crying didn't change the past or solve my problems but it was indeed a good release!

* * *

Light and Free!🖤

WHAT PRICE YOU PAY?

The truth of the matter is declaring that God is bringing about new seasons of growth, and all the new doors of opportunities and change are all scary!

* * *

… because there is no such thing as something for nothing. We all get to pay the price, somehow.

WHAT DO YOU EMBRACE?

F unny but with self-reflection, comes change.

For things I have control of, I learned to confront… and not backbite. There wasn't just any sense in letting all the people in the world know about what I was feeling and get sympathy when the person concerned was clueless!

What for, right? For me, it was much better to confront because I get the results I want at once!

For things I have no control of, I learned to embrace. I've learned to let go and give it to the person, situation, and life. KARMA isn't sleeping anyway.

* * *

In learning to change my thoughts, I had changed my life. 🖤

WHAT DO YOU HEAR?

Sometimes, a dream is born, because of serendipity. Sometimes, you don't even wish for it, and yet the opportunity is just there for you to grab. When your inner voice tells you to be it, or do it, or have it, listen.

* * *

And life will never be the same again.

WHAT MAKES YOU SAD?

I've always loved Desiderata.

"Go placidly amidst the noise and haste, and remember what peace there may be in silence. As far as possible without surrender, be on good terms with all persons…"

Our 6th grade teacher made us memorize it, and in a very good way, it has been words to live by.

The last verse says:

Therefore be at peace with God, whatever you conceive Him to be. And whatever your labors and aspirations, in the noisy confusion of life, keep peace in your soul. With all its sham, drudgery, and broken dreams, it is still a beautiful world. Be cheerful. **Strive to be happy.**"

In wanting to have more, we sometimes forget to be thankful for what we do have… and that's sad.

It is sad when we allow all the material possessions and it is sad if we get too attached to our future and dark imaginings.

It is sad to live out of fear, anxieties, and worries because we do not acknowledge the gift of today, our present.

It is sad if we continuously confine ourselves to our own boxes we forget to stretch, reach out, and move out of our own solitary places.

It is sad if we allow ourselves to be defined by our past and be trapped to resentment, resistance, and revenge.

It is sad because we are choosing to hold on to our own high ideals, pride, and righteousness we couldn't surrender to great possibilities.

It is sad that we can't wake up in the morning with a smile on our faces because God woke us up to live another day.

It is sad that we don't appreciate the air that we breathe, the water we drink, the food we eat…

It is sad that I can go on and on of things we could be happy about but choose not to see, hear, or feel.

* * *

Be grateful. Be happy.

WHAT'S YOUR ADVENTURE?

I enjoy going through this writing process time and time again – more than the finished work.

I think it's the same joy that the cooks go through in their cooking journey, painters go through in painting or dishwashers while washing the dishes. When we see work, not as a routine and obligation, but a joyful adventure, it makes the difference. Suddenly, creative art comes to life!

If we become less attached to the final product, and "just do it!" we become more imaginative. We can even risk deeper and try new things!

If we become less attached to the outcome, life surprises us!

And if we become less attached to what other people will say, wouldn't life be happier?

* * *

Cheers! 🖤

WHAT MATTERS?

I love that we always have a choice — to find our own path, to find our own voice, to find our own joy... at our own time, pace, and space.

Always remember, YOU matter.

* * *

But what matters most is the whisper of God in our hearts — telling us that the present is the precious gift!

WHAT ARE YOUR CHALLENGES?

I f nothing is a coincidence and everything is for a purpose, then I thank God for 2020.

Although I'm ready to bid it goodbye, 2020 is a major eye-opener for me.

I talked to one of the teachers who we've helped in Teach-USA, and he said my experience with Teach-USA felt like the water poured down on me, and then it's gone. And I added while I just "shampooed" my hair! And we both laughed.

I left my employer to work on the employment facilitation agency to help teachers teach in the US. And with the pandemic, everything came to a halt. In hindsight, I knew the permanency of the business would be dependent on governmental agencies. And sadly, the pessimistic vision revealed itself this 2020.

Although all decisions are temporary, I am grateful for our yield, and the many changed lives because of the agency.

All through the months of "hiding," I am thankful for the many hidden gems that surfaced. I believe it is true that the grace of God abounds in the deepest waters.

The teacher and I laughed at our analogy with the flow of water. But, on the contrary, the flow didn't stop. It merely changed settings.

The adjustments, changes, and shifts are all worthy and necessary to allow the possibility of the grander vision to come true!

Come what may, the best is yet to come, and all is well.

Let's all keep the faith alive!

* * *

Through You alone, O Lord, will I find my peace.

WHAT ARE YOU READY FOR?

When we open our doors to opportunities, it brings about change and change is wonderful!

Change will change your world!

Change will stretch your mind to new possibilities.

Change will take you to heights to which you've never been before.

* * *

So, what do you think? Are you ready for some change in your life? 🖤

ABOUT THE AUTHOR

Gemma is the author of the books "Believe It to See It: Dreams Do Come True", "Together Forever: 25 Lessons to Happily Ever After", and co-authored a book with Bo Sanchez and Sha Nacino, "To the First Woman Who Loved Me".

She is a *cum laude* graduate of Bachelor in Secondary Education major in Computer Technology at the University of Santo Tomas in Manila, Philippines, and a graduate of Master in Science Teaching at the New Mexico Institute of Mining and Technology in New Mexico, USA.

She is a miracle-believer, life-long learner, and a "dreams-do-come-true" advocate.

Please check out her website at https://www.gemsdaily.com and get to know her more at https://www. gemmahilotin.com.

BOOKS BY GEMMA

Gemma's books are available on Amazon.

To The First Woman Who Loved Me is available by request.

AFTERWORD

I took this photo when they released the white balloons at Mommy Grace's burial. It was sideways when I took the picture, but when flipped, we saw this image!

It was a beautiful cloud formation - I believe God was welcoming my Mommy back in His arms!

After a while, the rainbow appeared.🩶